"God's Own Child is a three-session l   ~~~paration program for parents. Very practical and pastoral in its approach and content, it treats adults as mature, responsible Christians. The program promotes personal interaction between parish staff and parents through interviews, and it stimulates communication between parents with worksheets and discussion questions. *God's Own Child* is easy to use and flexible; it is suitable for groups or individual sets of parents. An explanation of the baptism ceremony is provided, along with the counseling sessions.

"In this program parents will be challenged to think, communicate, and take stock of their feelings, beliefs, and values. It will also help them renew their own faith."

Sr. Alice Doll
St. Cloud Visitor

"What a gift this book is to the faith life of families! Not only is *God's Own Child* useful in preparing for a child's baptism, but the information and advice on what it means to be a Christian will serve parents well throughout their children's growing-up years."

Mary Carol Kendzia
Editor, *Growing Faith, Growing Family* newsletter

"God's Own Child encourages parental involvement in the rite, providing solid, updated liturgical information and a complete section on preparing for the ceremony. The section on family preparation for baptism is worth the price of the whole book.

"This program gives an exciting thrust to the significance of being a Christian parent. Some of the material on symbol catechesis is the most complete available."

Modern Liturgy

"The occasion of an infant's baptism is the perfect opportunity for the parents to reaffirm their own faith. *God's Own Child* offers the perfect timing for this. But because there are so many demands on the parish staff's time, not everyone is prepared to give a dynamic class, and then repeat it every week. This manual for the parents and leader's guide are the perfect answer.

"This large-sized book has plenty of working space and is invaluable as a pastoral aid, one that is easy to recommend highly."

Msgr. Charles Dollen
The Priest

"I find *God's Own Child* to be practical and pastoral in its approach and content, refreshing in its vision, and geared to treat adults as mature responsible Christians."

Jody Sinwell
Director of Religious Education
Providence, R.I.

"This book is designed with three sessions to be used in the parish with groups of parents preparing for the baptism of their children. With suggestions for individual counseling sessions, it also includes information about the ceremony of baptism and ways a parish can respond to the parents' need to prepare for it through a revitalization of their own faith."

Religious Education Newsletter
Diocese of Belleville

"God's Own Child is a pre-baptism program that comes to grips with the real needs of parents about to baptize their child. Here is a book that recognizes the confusion of many young Catholic parents and talks to them about personal faith and their church."

Pastor
Charlotte, N.C.

BILL AND PATTY COLEMAN

GOD'S OWN CHILD

A BOOK FOR PARENTS WELCOMING THEIR CHILD
INTO THE CHRISTIAN COMMUNITY

XXIII
TWENTY-THIRD PUBLICATIONS
Mystic, Connecticut 06355

English translation of excerpts from the Rite of Baptism for Children
© 1969, International Committee for English in the Liturgy, Inc.
All rights reserved.

Fourth Printing of Revised Edition 1998

Twenty-Third Publications
185 Willow Street
P.O. Box 180
Mystic, CT 06355
(860) 536-2611
800-321-0411

ISBN 0-89622-652-2
Library of Congress Catalog Card Number 95-60062
Printed in the U.S.A.

DEDICATION

For our grandchildren,
God's very own children
and the apple of our eyes.

Contents

PART ONE
God and the Church

PART TWO
God and Sin

PART THREE
Becoming a Christian Parent

PART FOUR
Preparing for the Ceremony

A Note from Your Friends at

_____
(Parish)

Dear Parents,

Congratulations!

We are looking forward to welcoming your child into the Christian community through baptism. We want to share your joy and that of your family, your friends, and your child's godparents. Soon your very own child will be marked with the sign of the cross and made a member of God's family.

Because baptism is such a memorable moment in your life and in that of all your family and friends, we would like to talk with you and explain what we can about the life of faith, the church, and the sacrament itself.

To prepare for your child's baptism, we ask you to:

1. Read this book together with that special adult who shares your life of faith most deeply. Ideally, that person will be your husband or wife, but not always, since today many parents must raise their children by themselves, or their mate has little interest in religious matters.

   No matter whom you choose as your discussion partner, what is important is that you delve deeply into your own faith. To do that, it will be important to discuss your beliefs and hopes with each other, and pray with someone who will understand you and your search for a living faith that will guide you through life's turmoil.

   In *God's Own Child* you will find information and answers to many questions that today's Catholic parents are asking. We hope it will start you thinking about your own faith and help you better understand what advantages you already have to pass on to your child.

2. Note the meetings we will have together. The dates, times, and locations are given below.

Again, we are looking forward to sharing this happy event with you. For further information, call _____ at _____.

Please bring your copy of *God's Own Child* to the meetings.

MEETINGS

DATE	TIME	LOCATION
1. _____	_____	_____
2. _____	_____	_____
3. _____	_____	_____

Baptism Record

"Think of the love that God has lavished on us, by letting us be called God's own children; and that is what we are." 1 John 3:1

_____   _____
Father's name   Mother's maiden name

in a spirit of faithful love presented their child

_____
Name

to the Christian community,
which joyfully welcomed this child
into the family of God
through the rite of solemn baptism on

_____
Date

_____   _____
Parish   Priest or Deacon

_____   _____
Godfather   Godmother

_____   _____
City   State

Introduction

Welcome

Your own child! What a wonder! What a miracle life is!

Whether you are raising your child alone or with the person you love, whether you gave birth to the child or through adoption promised to give it new life, whether your child is an infant or already exploring the wide new world, whether your own faith is strong or you are just beginning to make it your own, whether you and your husband or wife share the same religious background or come from very different religious traditions, you have a child! That is the miracle, and you are welcome here.

All About Love

A young king once asked a wise man, "What is the greatest gift I can give my child?" The wise man replied, "Love the child's mother." A love that binds parents together or supports a parent who is called to raise a child alone is the greatest need any child has.

That love on which the child's security rests should also go beyond parents' love for each other. It should reach out to grandparents, aunts, uncles, and cousins, and beyond to God and to the church, the community of the faithful. All have a part in strengthening and affirming this new life. The wider the community of family and friends and the closer the bond to God and the Christian community, the deeper will be the support and strength your child will have now and in every phase of life.

Your Decision

Times have changed. A few generations ago, couples seldom thought seriously of divorce, of not remaining close to their parents, or of not remaining a part of their church. Divorce was rare, family neglect unthinkable, and being without a church, a social disgrace.

Life today is different. Carl Jung, the Swiss psychoanalyst, said that the mark of being "modern" is making our own decisions. You decide whether you will remain married or not. You decide how close you will be to your extended family. You even decide how closely you will live with God and with the church into which you were born. Whatever decisions you make, for good or bad, will profoundly affect your lives and the life of your child.

The first concrete religious decision you make for your child is about baptism. The fact that you are reading this book probably means that you have already decided to have your child baptized. Congratulations! For a variety of reasons, some old and some very new, you have made a wise decision.

Family Affair

Besides being a church ceremony, baptism has always been a family affair. It marks a special moment in the lives of parents and provides an opportunity for the entire family to share the joy of the occasion and to welcome the child into the web of relationships which is the extended family.

In a sense, baptism can be the child's first birthday party. If there were no sacrament of welcome and incorporation into the church for children, people would have to invent something like it because they need an opportunity to celebrate the child's arrival and to welcome the child into the "flesh and blood" family and into the wider community of believers.

This family is an attractive reason to baptize one's child. Many, however, feel that it is not enough, that there must be other, deeper reasons, too. And such reasons exist.

Church Affair

To understand our deepest reasons for infant baptism, we might well turn to the baptism ceremony itself. In the very beginning of the ceremony, the priest asks the parents, "What do you ask of the church?" The parents reply, "Faith." Everyone knows that the church cannot give faith. Faith is God's free gift. Yet the church can and does create the atmosphere in which faith is more likely to be nurtured and develop. It can give the child a variety of experiences and a web of relationships in which faith will flower in due time.

The Christian community promises that it will be a part of the child's daily life through its rituals, its service, its concern, and its imperfect but struggling spiritual life. At baptism the child becomes a part of this pilgrim community. For better or for worse, the child is bound to the men and women who struggle to worship God through Jesus, God's son.

God's Role

But so far we have spoken only about people. What about God? Saint Paul tells us that baptism is a kind of adoption ceremony in which the child becomes a younger brother or sister of Jesus. This new relationship freely given by God allows the child to turn to God in confidence and say, "Abba, Daddy." Because we think of God today as both masculine and feminine, we can call God "mother" as well. So close is the relationship between the baptized and God that the child becomes a son or daughter of God, not merely a creature.

This adoption is a free gift of God, who has loved us first and loves us so intensely that we are impelled to act as God's children. God does not demand that we first act properly and then love us, any more than parents would demand that their children first be well behaved and then they would be loved.

Reasons for Baptism

Why do you want your child to be baptized? Your reasons may be many. You may never question the practice of baptizing children, or you may want to have your child baptized because it is expected. You may have lingering fears about "original sin." You may want your family to have a special day to honor your child. You may sense that in these tempestuous times your child will need a community of faith in which to grow. You may understand that baptism, like other sacraments, is a touch of the divine in the life of your child.

All of these are good reasons, some more profound than others, but all good in their way. Later in your life you may come to understand and appreciate some of the reasons that today mean little to you. Life is like that. We continue to grow in our understanding and in our faith, just as our children grow in grace and wisdom and age.

PART ONE

God and the Church

From the Ceremony . . .

Dear parents and godparents: You have come here to present [this child] for baptism. By water and the Holy Spirit [he (she)] is to receive the gift of new life from God, who is love.

On your part, you must make it your constant care to bring [this child] up in the practice of the faith. See that the divine life which God gives [him (her)] is kept safe from the poison of sin, to grow always stronger in [his (her)] heart.

If your faith makes you ready to accept this responsibility, renew now the vows of your own baptism. Reject sin; profess your faith in Christ Jesus. This is the faith of the Church. This is the faith in which [this child is] about to be baptized.

—from the invitation to parents to profess their faith

Celebrant:	Do you believe in God, the Father almighty, creator of heaven and earth?
Parents and Godparents:	I do.
Celebrant:	Do you believe in Jesus Christ, his only son, our Lord, who was born of the Virgin Mary, was crucified, died, and was buried, rose from the dead, and is now seated at the right hand of the Father?
Parents and Godparents:	I do.
Celebrant:	Do you believe in the Holy Spirit, the holy catholic Church, the communion of saints, the forgiveness of sins, the resurrection of the body, and life everlasting?
Parents and Godparents:	I do.
Celebrant:	This is our faith. This is the faith of the Church. We are proud to profess it, in Christ Jesus our Lord.
All:	Amen.

—from the profession of faith that parents make before their child is baptized

Faith and the Church

To focus your thoughts . . .

Please indicate whether you agree or disagree with each statement on this page. Ask your partner to do the same on the page that follows. Both pages are identical. Please do this without discussing the statements. When you have each completed your own set of responses, compare your answers with those of your partner and discuss your agreements and disagreements.

1. My faith is something personal. It is mine. I am responsible for it to no one but God.

___Agree   ___Disagree

2. Faith is going to church, obeying the laws, and believing what the church teaches.

___Agree   ___Disagree

3. My faith is from my family. I belong to the church because they did. I believe because they did.

___Agree   ___Disagree

4. For me, God is as real as my parents. God is always with me.

___Agree   ___Disagree

5. The church is as much a part of faith as God is.

___Agree   ___Disagree

6. The church is important to me. I would not know how to live without it.

___Agree   ___Disagree

7. My real problem of faith is not with God, but with the church.

___Agree   ___Disagree

8. I wish the church were more spiritual. I wish it did more to help me know and love God.

        ___Agree   ___Disagree

9. The church is its members, people like me who are not perfect but are trying.

        ___Agree   ___Disagree

10. I am not sure whether I am a member of the church any more. I wish I knew, but I am honestly not sure any more.

        ___Agree   ___Disagree

After your discussion, read together the following essays on faith and the church, pages 13–17.

Faith and the Church

To focus your thoughts . . .

Please indicate whether you agree or disagree with each statement on this page. Ask your partner to do the same on her page. Both pages are identical. Please do this without discussing the statements. When you have each completed your own set of responses, compare your answers with those of your partner and discuss your agreements and disagreements.

1. My faith is something personal. It is mine. I am responsible for it to no one but God.

      ___Agree   ___Disagree

2. Faith is going to church, obeying the laws, and believing what the church teaches.

      ___Agree   ___Disagree

3. My faith is from my family. I belong to the church because they did. I believe because they did.

      ___Agree   ___Disagree

4. For me, God is as real as my parents. God is always with me.

      ___Agree   ___Disagree

5. The church is as much a part of faith as God is.

      ___Agree   ___Disagree

6. The church is important to me. I would not know how to live without it.

      ___Agree   ___Disagree

7. My real problem of faith is not with God, but with the church.

      ___Agree   ___Disagree

8. I wish the church were more spiritual. I wish it did more to help me know and love God.

        ___Agree   ___Disagree

9. The church is its members, people like me who are not perfect but are trying.

        ___Agree   ___Disagree

10. I am not sure whether I am a member of the church any more. I wish I knew, but I am honestly not sure any more.

        ___Agree   ___Disagree

After your discussion, read together the following essays on faith and the church, pages 13–17.

Faith

 What is this faith of ours? It is certainly more than a set of abstract beliefs. It is a deep personal relationship with Jesus, a kind of lifestyle that springs from our conviction that God is our father and our mother and that Jesus is our brother.

Faith transforms lives. It adds joy, peace, closeness to the Lord, and patience to the mix of comings and goings we call our daily lives. It is like salt; its flavor is almost taken for granted until we find ourselves without it. This faith is so essential to living happily that no gift a parent can share with a child is more important.

Always Unique

That lifestyle may be hard to put into words, for each person lives faith a little differently. Some are full of fire, as Saint Paul was. Their lives are profoundly changed by an inner experience, and they then set out to share that experience with anyone who will listen. Others live out their faith in a more placid way. They have that peace of heart promised to those who believe, and everything about them speaks peace. Saint John and Mary herself seemed to be like that.

Whether we are like Saint Paul, Saint John, or Mary, whether we are fiery or placid, there is something special about us when we are people of faith. That specialness is, of course, a close personal friendship with the Lord.

Always Deeply Personal

One writer has said, "God has no grandchildren." What he meant is that every Christian person must make faith his or her own. No one inherits faith from another generation. Faith is always a personal reality; there is nothing automatic about it. It grows only when an individual accepts it, for faith is very much like love. We experience love only when we allow ourselves to notice the people in our lives who care for us.

This intensely personal dimension of faith is what many discover only when they are in adult life. After living for years in a faith-filled family, going to Mass each Sunday, and even attending a school in which religion was a daily concern, they find that they still do not have a personal faith. Then, at some crisis moment in their young lives, they decide for or against a personal and living faith.

No one can believe for another any more than one can love for another. Faith is uniquely personal, so much so that it profoundly influences the inner life of believers and shapes their personality as much as does the family or a love affair.

Psychologists of religion chart the many stages that a person raised in the church goes through as he or she matures and develops a deeply personal faith. These stages are not unlike those found in the development of a friendship. In childhood, friendships are taken for granted. There is little reflection or personal decision about them. Later in life, reflection comes and, with it, a great tentativeness about all relationships. Finally, in adult life a friendship becomes both reflective and complete.

Some Christians put such emphasis on this personal dimension of faith that they defer baptism until it has been achieved. The Catholic Christian tradition, while recognizing the goal of personal faith, still believes in the ancient practice of making infants members of its community, acknowledging that the best place to discover personal faith is within that community.

Here the child experiences the sacraments, learns about the Bible, takes part in prayer, witnesses the faith-life of believing adults, and benefits from all the other aids to a personal awakening to Jesus.

Always within a Family

For most Christians, faith is rooted in a family experience. Most learn about Jesus not in a classroom, but in the words and deeds of parents and other believing adults. From them children learn that God exists, what it means to be a Christian, and what God has done through the long history of our human family. The first—and most important—teacher of the word of God is not the parish priest, the bishop, or the pope, but parents who believe.

Faith is, then, a family affair, not in its ultimate acceptance—which is essentially personal—but in its beginnings. It is this family-centeredness of faith that the church celebrates in each child's baptism. It is here that the priest asks the child's parents to state their own beliefs and to promise to help their child reach the fullness of adult faith.

Always within the Church

Besides being personal and family-rooted, faith is always tied to the church. It is true that all the church-going in the world will not induce faith. It is also true that many who attend church and participate in its programs and rites are not, for that reason, mature believers.

Still, faith does rely heavily upon the church. Sociologists tell us that the church is a kind of reference group for believers. It believes that a decision to follow Jesus is sane and wise. It strengthens the resolve of believers and helps them understand that life with faith can be and is a great adventure.

Children are introduced to Jesus not only by their parents, but also by observing kindly people who love them. They learn prayer by watching people praying at church as well as at home. They learn what it means to serve others by listening to the stories of those who have spent their lives serving other people in simple—and sometimes heroic—ways. They learn the traditions of the church and the wonders expressed in the Bible both from their parents and from those in the church who teach them.

Final Word

Faith is always personal but lived in the family and the church. We grow from an *unreflective* acceptance of a way of life to a troubled but *reflective* period in our teens, and only later enter into a total and completely *personal* faith. Infant baptism marks the beginning of our quest.

This invitation to be part of the Christian community is now open to your child. Through you, your family, and the church, God reaches out to your child and says, "I will be with you every day, for I shall be your Parent and you shall be my child. With your family and the church to help you, you will begin your quest for a faith that will bring you joy here and in the life to come."

The Church

 The church is people at prayer, in service to others, and in a search for a deeper understanding of the Lord. By observing the people of God on their pilgrimage, children are inspired to search for the faith that transforms mediocrity into greatness.

Your child will be baptized into the church. The whole community of believers will take on a new relationship with this child. Suddenly your child will have a very large family of aunts and uncles, cousins and kin. As long as your family opens themselves to these new relationships, none of you will ever be alone.

New Family

Theologians call it a community, a group of people who share the same history, love the same symbols, and care about the same goals and ideals. This means that a community is a kind of large family. Like any family, it has its good moments and its bad, but its bonds are always present in our lives. No matter what happens to us, this family, like most families, is always ready to welcome us back and to love us without question.

Ecumenical Family

Sadly, we followers of Jesus have not always lived in peace and harmony with one another. Over the centuries our ancestors have quarreled over what to believe, how to worship, how the church should be organized, and which actions are good and which are bad. Yet, there is something profound that binds us together, for all Christians believe in the same God and in Jesus who became brother of us all.

Before all else, your child will be baptized into this great ecumenical family of faith. Your task as parents is to teach your child to love and respect all who believe in Jesus and to understand that whatever differences may separate us, our deepest bond of faith makes us one family even when we fail to understand it.

Catholic Family

We Catholics are a special part of that great ecumenical family. We are bound together by a special history. For centuries, men and women like us have struggled together in their quest for personal faith. Some of them have been great saints. Many more have lived quite ordinary lives marked by their desire to love and serve others.

As Catholics, we are also bound together by our love of the same religious traditions: our symbols, the Mass, the sacraments, the Bible, the sign of the cross, the Lord's Prayer, and so many other day-to-day realities of our religious lives. We take these symbols for granted and are comfortable with one another in using them.

Even more profound is the bond of a belief that binds us into a single family. While we may disagree about many things, we all share a belief in the central meaning of life itself and in God's concern for us. We believe that God is, that God loves us, that Jesus is our human brother, that all of us matter in the divine plan of things.

Bound together by our history, our symbols, and our beliefs, we form a large family. This is the family that opens its arms and hearts to your child. It promises that there will always be a place in the life of the church for this special child.

Community of Prayer

Your child's new family will gather often to give praise to the Father. Each Sunday people all over the world will come together to raise their hearts to God in prayer and ritual. That prayer will be full of thanks for life's blessings, praise for the greatness of the giver of all blessings, sorrow over their own shortcomings, and petitions for a better life ahead.

You and your child will be a part of this prayer. Even when you forget to pray, some members of your church family will remember you. That bond of prayer will be unbroken.

Community of Service

Jesus told his disciples that only those who fed the hungry, gave drink to the thirsty, clothed the naked, visited the imprisoned, and genuinely cared about others would be rewarded in heaven. He also said that those who failed to do these things failed to minister to him when he was poor and homeless (Matthew 25:31–46).

For this reason, the church is always a community of service. Its members open their lives and their fortunes to others. Some do this as missionaries in foreign lands. Others open their wallets and offer to support worthwhile projects. Still others work among the poor and powerless in their own towns and cities. Service is always a part of the Christian commitment. When it is not present, the true church of Jesus is not yet formed.

Community of Searchers

One medieval saint said that faith always seeks understanding. Once we have come to believe, we want to know more about Jesus, his Father, and the community of which we are a part. We look for a deeper understanding of the words and ideas that guide our Catholic understanding of God. We try to learn about the great men and women who have already lived the Christian life and about the times in which they made their own pilgrimages. We want to learn about the biblical record of the early church and of the generations of people who went before them. We want to delve more deeply into the everyday meaning of the sacraments and the ritual life of the community.

Because our faith is always deepening, so too is our desire to understand more and more about God and the things of God. This makes of us a community in search of understanding.

Beyond Community

All communities must be organized and orderly. When they are not, they quickly disintegrate. Members take advantage of other members and are moved to and fro by personal enthusiasms. Without organization, a community dies.

The Catholic community is organized. Some fear that the organizational aspect of our Christian life may at times be too clear-cut and too demanding. Yet without that organization we would soon splinter into conflicting and troubled factions.

Briefly, we believe that the fundamental building block of our community is the bishop. When he and his people are gathered together in peace, the fullness of church is present. Because there are so many members of the community, the bishop is assisted by ministers we call priests. They gather together with parts of the community into what we call parishes. These parishes are united under the bishop.

Bishops themselves represent their local churches by gathering together and exchanging ideas and visions. From their number, one bishop is chosen to be the focus of their unity. That bishop is the Bishop of Rome, the person we call pope. He is the focus of the worldwide unity of the church. He enhances that unity by sharing with all Catholic Christians ideas and expectations that give a uniformity to Catholic Christianity everywhere.

Most Catholics experience church only at the parish level. Here they discover the community, united with their pastor, struggling to be a people of prayer, service, and learning. Sometimes that struggle seems successful, but at other times there is more strife and imperfection than seems necessary.

Realizing that the church is people, and therefore imperfect, will go a long way in helping us accept the church as we find it. If it is less than it should be, that is because we have not yet given it enough of ourselves, our gifts, and our desire to make it the community God intended.

Final Word

We do not believe in the church as we believe in God. There is only one God and God alone is worthy of our worship. Yet we do believe the church, for it is credible and worthy of our belief. When it is less than it should be, we struggle as part of it to make it more clearly the sign of the love of God in our world.

Into this church your child is welcomed and will always be a part of its prayers, its service to the poor, its searching. With all its imperfections and uncertainties, the church will be your child's second family: aunts, uncles, and cousins bound together in this world and in the next.

Ideas for Prayer and Pondering

The short essays that follow are not an essential part of the baptism preparation for parents. You may, however, enjoy reading them to gain a more complete knowledge of topics related to baptism and the Christian life.

Baptism—Historical Sketch

From the earliest times baptism has been a part of the initiation into Christian life. Immediately after Pentecost, the apostles preached to all who would listen about the life, death, and resurrection of Jesus. Those who believed asked what they should do. Peter answered, "You must repent and every one of you must be baptized in the name of Jesus Christ for the forgiveness of your sins" (Acts 2:38).

Obviously, Peter was speaking to adults, for only adults can repent. Nothing is said here about children but a few chapters later in the Acts of the Apostles, Peter met the family of Cornelius, a pagan official who also believed in Jesus (Acts 10:1–11:18) and baptized his whole family, men, women, and children.

All Christians agree that there are three stages in accepting Jesus: believing in him, changing our lives, and being baptized. Not

all are sure what is the best order to follow. Should baptism be postponed until adulthood so that believing and reordering our lives always come before baptism as happened at Pentecost? Or, should baptism take place in infancy so that children awaken gradually to a personal belief in Jesus and develop a willingness to change and renew their lives, as happened with the family of Cornelius? The Catholic church has practiced infant baptism for centuries and recommends this to today's parents.

Baptism originally was an immersion, plunging the whole person into water while saying "I baptize you . . ." Early churches contained a baptism pool which those to be baptized entered for the ceremony. As the church spread into colder climates and began to baptize more and more people, many pastors abandoned the pools and simply poured water on the foreheads of those they baptized. The meaning, or symbolism, they felt, was still quite clear.

During the third and fourth centuries in Rome, those who were to be baptized spent the whole season of Lent preparing for their entry into the church. They received instruction in the faith and attended Mass but were dismissed after the homily and not allowed to participate in the most sacred part of the ceremony. During the Easter Vigil, which is a celebration not only of the resurrection of Jesus but of our own resurrection with him through baptism, they were baptized and entered fully into the life of the Christian community.

In some countries today, such as Spain, infants are confirmed at the same time they are baptized, a very ancient custom, while in Northern European and American lands, we postpone confirmation until later.

All these historical developments are interesting and help us grasp the importance of each of the three stages necessary to enter adult Christian life: belief in Jesus, radical conversion of our lives, and baptism. What is most important, though, is not the way we accomplish this, but the reality and sincerity of our faith and our Christ-like lives.

Baptism—A Beginning

Faith, like love, must be constantly renewed or the cares of daily life will snuff it out. In a sense, all the sacraments are a renewal of our baptism. Each of them helps us refocus our faith at a crucial moment in our lives: entry into young adult life, marriage, ordination, times of serious illness, times when we need forgiveness, and especially our regular meetings with Jesus in the Eucharist.

Tied closely to the sacraments is the liturgy of the church. Each year all of us are called to renew our baptism faith during the season of Lent. Each week of Lent the liturgy asks us to ponder some of the most powerful passages in the Bible and then, after a reflective six weeks, to renew and celebrate our baptism faith during the Easter Vigil Mass.

The liturgy and the sacraments are important opportunities to renew our faith. There are other moments, too, moments of deep personal stress: disappointments with those close to us, crises in our working life, discoveries of betrayal, times of depression and anguish, confronting illness and death. These are the times when nothing but faith can carry us on, and faith itself seems clouded over by our trouble. It is from these depths of sadness and confusion that we call to God with an uncertain voice.

In such crises, faith is tempered and made strong. Often God is closest to us when we feel most abandoned and alone.

Talking Together

The purpose of this page is to stimulate discussion. An identical sheet is provided for each discussion partner. It is done best after reading all of Part One.

1. Experiences in my life that remind me that my faith must be a personal thing:

_____

_____

_____

_____

2. Experiences in my life that remind me that my faith is rooted in my family:

_____

_____

_____

_____

3. Experiences in my life that remind me that my faith relies on the church:

_____

_____

_____

_____

Spend as much time as you can discussing your answers together (after completing the sheets). Try to understand not only what your partner thinks, but how he feels. Then take a few moments to pray together about what you discovered in your discussion.

_____

Talking Together

The purpose of this page is to stimulate discussion. An identical sheet is provided for each discussion partner. It is done best after reading all of Part One.

1. Experiences in my life that remind me that my faith must be a personal thing:

_____

_____

_____

_____

2. Experiences in my life that remind me that my faith is rooted in my family:

_____

_____

_____

_____

3. Experiences in my life that remind me that my faith relies on the church:

_____

_____

_____

_____

Spend as much time as you can discussing your answers together (after completing the sheets). Try to understand not only what your partner thinks, but how she feels. Then take a few moments to pray together about what you discovered in your discussion.

PART TWO

God and Sin

From the Ceremony . . .

People were bringing little children to him for him to touch them. The disciples turned them away, but when Jesus saw this he was indignant and said to them, "Let the little children come to me; do not stop them; for it is to such as these that the kingdom of God belongs. I tell you solemnly, anyone who does not welcome the kingdom of God like a little child will never enter it." Then he put his arms round them, laid his hands on them and gave them his blessing.

Mark 10:13–16, a reading often used in the baptism ceremony

Celebrant: Do you reject sin, so as to live in the freedom of God's children?

Parents and
Godparents: I do.

Celebrant: Do you reject the glamor of evil, and refuse to be mastered by sin?

Parents and
Godparents: I do.

Celebrant: Do you reject Satan, father of sin and prince of darkness?

Parents and
Godparents: I do.

—from the rejection of sin made by the parents before the child's baptism.

God and Sin

To focus your thoughts . . .

Please indicate whether you agree or disagree with each statement on this page. Ask your partner to do the same on the page that follows. Both pages are identical. Please do this without discussing the statements. When you have each completed your own set of responses, compare your answers with those of your partner and discuss your agreements and disagreements.

1. God keeps an accurate record of our every thought, word, and deed and punishes us for every deviation from God's law.

_____Agree   _____Disagree

2. God is kind, gentle, and willing to accept us the way we are.

_____Agree   _____Disagree

3. God's laws are to help people be just and happy, not to make them feel guilty and afraid.

_____Agree   _____Disagree

4. God seems more understanding and more forgiving than the church does.

_____Agree   _____Disagree

5. Each person understands God in a different way. No one knows what God is really like.

_____Agree   _____Disagree

6. Whenever we knowingly disobey the laws of God or the church, we commit a sin.

_____Agree   _____Disagree

7. Sin is a failure to care about other people. Doing nothing for others can be a greater sin than breaking a rule.

_____Agree   _____Disagree

8. I find it hard to believe an innocent child is in original sin.

        ____Agree   ____Disagree

9. I don't know that personal sin is so important. War, injustice, and violence are the real evils in the world.

        ____Agree   ____Disagree

10. I never think about sin any more. I suppose it exists and I suppose I commit it, but somehow I never think much about it.

        ____Agree   ____Disagree

After your discussion, read together the following essay on our ideas about God and sin.

God and Sin

To focus your thoughts . . .

Please indicate whether you agree or disagree with each statement on this page. Ask your partner to do the same on her page. Both pages are identical. Please do this without discussing the statements. When you have each completed your own set of responses, compare your answers with those of your partner and discuss your agreements and disagreements.

1. God keeps an accurate record of our every thought, word, and deed and punishes us for every deviation from God's law.

    ____Agree   ____Disagree

2. God is kind, gentle, and willing to accept us the way we are.

    ____Agree   ____Disagree

3. God's laws are to help people be just and happy, not to make them feel guilty and afraid.

    ____Agree   ____Disagree

4. God seems more understanding and more forgiving than the church does.

    ____Agree   ____Disagree

5. Each person understands God in a different way. No one knows what God is really like.

    ____Agree   ____Disagree

6. Whenever we knowingly disobey the laws of God or the church, we commit a sin.

    ____Agree   ____Disagree

7. Sin is a failure to care about other people. Doing nothing for others can be a greater sin than breaking a rule.

    ____Agree   ____Disagree

8. I find it hard to believe an innocent child is in original sin.

        ____Agree   ____Disagree

9. I don't know that personal sin is so important. War, injustice, and violence are the real evils in the world.

        ____Agree   ____Disagree

10. I never think about sin any more. I suppose it exists and I suppose I commit it, but somehow I never think much about it.

        ____Agree   ____Disagree

After your discussion, read together the following essay on our ideas about God and sin.

Images of God

What is God like? There is no one answer to this for everyone because, as Saint Paul said, now we see unclearly as in an imperfect mirror. Thus each of us knows God differently. For the strong and stern, God seems mighty and powerful. For the gentle and loving, God is love. All people give to the word "God" something of their own personality.

Bible Images

The Bible contains many different images of God. In the days of Moses, for example, God stood on the mountain engraving his commands in tablets of stone. To disobey these commands was to die. The Old Testament prophet Amos came to the court of Israel to preach a vision of a fierce and fiery God. Yet for the prophet Hosea, God was faithful, never hostile, infinitely patient, ever loyal. The Bible's wisdom books describe God with all the tenderness, compassion, and sensitivity that people of that age associated with a woman, and God's faithful love is nowhere more evident than in the story of Ruth.

In the gospels Jesus spoke of his Father and told us that God is our Father, too. He told the story of the prodigal son who found his father full of tenderness and understanding, patiently waiting for him to return from the fleshpots of the city. Even with his inheritance squandered, the prodigal found a welcome with his forgiving parent. Yet Jesus himself also spoke of God destroying the cities of the unrepentant and sounded ominous as he spoke of the sheep and the goats on judgment day.

What all these biblical images of God tell us is that God is viewed differently by different people; even the same person may

have several images of God. God is like a father and like a mother, too, but neither image is complete, for God is mystery. No one grasps God's true personality. The closest we can come to understanding God is to study the life and attitudes of Jesus. He told us that anyone who has seen him has already seen the Father.

Jesus, Perfect Image

What was Jesus like? The overwhelming impression one gains from the New Testament stories of Jesus is that of a compassionate person of great personal strength. Jesus was a person of conviction, one who knew the truth and stood with that truth, whatever the consequences. Yet, Jesus had about him nothing of the fanatic's devotion to some abstract truth.

Jesus could sense the personal tragedy of the woman at the well and the embarrassment of the woman taken in adultery. He could forgive Peter's repeated lapses and brought forgiveness to Magdalen, Peter, and later to Paul. It was he who raised the widow's son to life and who wept at the death of his friend Lazarus.

Perhaps one might say of Jesus that he was so strong, so self-possessed, that he did not need to be harsh. He was so sure of himself and his grasp on the truth that he did not have to resort to power to protect himself or his message. Because he knew his truth was the truth and because his personality was fully mature, Jesus was able to behave calmly and remain in full possession of himself. His personal security was great enough to allow him to be gentle and kind.

Images of a Harsh God

Unfortunately, this is not the vision of God common among some Christian people. For them, God seems harsh, almost as cruel as the God of Moses' day, a God who delights in punishment and watches for the sinner's smallest error. This mistaken belief portrays God as one who punishes babies for the faults and negligences of their parents, who sends illness or earthquakes or famine on the land to satisfy an outraged sense of justice.

This harsh notion of God is more the creation of a neurosis than of the gospel. The form of neurosis that creates a despotic God begins with a feeling of self-hatred, perhaps because of errors inherited from childhood. When people hate themselves they are plagued by feelings of guilt. Only through punishment can this guilt be expiated. Guilt-ridden people need an avenging God, for only such a God can punish them and so relieve, for a time, the burden of their guilt. This self-hatred has created a terrible vision of God. Many good people, themselves well balanced, have been taught such a vision of God and have accepted it unthinkingly.

But this is not the vision of God found in the New Testament. The New Testament images, even when connected with punishment, give lie to this neurotic vision. They tell of a strong God, but one so self-possessed who has no need to reach out and destroy through punishment.

Images of an Indulgent God

With this said, we must not go to the opposite extreme and see in God one who does not care. God is not the indulgent parent afraid to enter into a confrontation with the children of God. God often shocks and challenges us, as all good parents do to help their children grow.

Jesus showed us this side of God's personality. He upbraided the scribes and Pharisees. He challenged the legalism of his day. He did not hesitate to challenge sinners and to call them to repentance. Yet Jesus spoke these strong words only to call the erring to repentance.

Final Word

All these images of God are only that—images. None of them contains the complete truth about God. They are all imperfect and incomplete. Just as we can never grasp the complete truth about another human personality so—even more—we cannot grasp the complete truth about the personality of God who is best described by Saint John: "God is love."

As his or her life unfolds, your child will discover more and more about this new Parent. You will help when you speak of God as kind and loving, never permissive, but never cruel or vindictive either. The more attractive you make God seem, the closer you will be to the truth and the more you will help your own child love and feel close to God who is the Father and Mother of us all.

Reality of Sin

 No one is more innocent than a little child. Yet the baptism ceremony speaks of sin and evil. At a moment when everyone is happy and full of joy, why bring up the unpleasant reality of sin? The reason is so simple that we may easily overlook it. Sin is a part of being human. Even the youngest among us is influenced by the sin of others. To deny the importance of sin in the life of the child is to forget that this child is fully human, a very real part of the ongoing life of our human race.

Sin is as much a part of daily life as zip code numbers. Understanding sin and its influence on us is important. Traditional theology calls three realities we all have encountered in our lives "sin." Though the words may seem archaic, the realities they represent are as present today as they were in medieval times.

Sin That Kills

There is a sin we call mortal, a kind of infection that destroys our human happiness and makes us hard, insensitive people, people so concerned with self that we have no time or energy left for others, including our family and our God.

Mortal, or to use its real name, "the sin that kills life in us," is the reality people first called sin. They saw much more than an isolated action forbidden by some law or set of ethical principles. Rather, this mortal sin was a way of life, an attitude of intense selfishness that blotted out any ability to care for others or for God.

Normally, this kind of sin does not happen all at once, just as a husband does not fall out of love with his wife in one fell swoop. Rather, his falling out of love is the accumulation of many smaller acts, the building of an attitude, one based on concerns that do not include his wife. So, too, mortal sinners do not awake in the friendship of God and suddenly, almost magically, fall from grace. Rather, they build toward a major change in life's moorings. When the building of this new and selfish attitude is complete, they may express it clearly and definitively in some terrible action that only serves to confirm what had already happened within them.

Young parents facing the dual challenge of raising a new child and making their way in the adult world face many decisions. They must decide how much of their energy will be spent on possessing a beautiful home and an expensive car. They must decide how much time they will spend together, how they will relate to their own parents, how they will help the needy, how they will fit into their parish.

Perhaps no one of these decisions is enough to mark their lives as deadened. But if many of these decisions are selfish, soon it will become clear that they have lost vitality and responsiveness. Soon it will be clear that they have destroyed the vitality of love in their married life. This deadening of consciousness and sensitivity is mortal sin. It destroys not only friendship with God, but what is really precious about human life itself, the ability to love.

Punishment of Sin

Does God punish this kind of sin? This is a deceptive question, one that leads to many strange visions of God. A very careful answer must be given. In a sense, God does punish sin because God presides over all the dynamics that control the course of human events in the world. God created the world and the world is God's.

But in a profound sense sin punishes itself. Sin, or selfishness, has an inner life of its own that leads to isolation and loneliness, to self-destruction and self-hatred. This inner life of sin destroys the sinners and even brings them to a point where they are so caught in the web of evil that they are unable or unwilling to turn their lives around.

This final state of being unable to move away from sin is, of course, what we Christians call hell. It is not so much that God creates hell and casts sinners into it, but that sinners so disfigure the human nature God has given them that they destroy the happiness they might have had. Sin is its own punishment.

Selfish Moments

There is another reality in life we also call sin, but it is so different from this mortal, or deadly, sin that we confuse ourselves by using the term "sin" at all. Ancient people noticed that even when the basic direction of their lives was decent and loving, there were many things that could be better. Husbands who loved their wives still behaved selfishly. Wives who loved their husbands still found themselves manipulating them in little things. These small acts of selfishness were troublesome. They showed the lack of integrity and consistency in human life. This inconsistency they began to call "the sin of the day" or "daily sin."

In time, theologians came to use another term for these shortcomings: "venial sin." The choice of this word was unfortunate, because it made people think that the condition of being so ingrown and selfish that one cannot love was almost the same as the little inconsistencies of daily life. Nothing could be further from the truth.

The sin that deadens the whole personality is so strong and so terrifying that it is a central fact of human life. The daily sins, the venial sins, while regrettable, are something quite different. They are on the periphery of human existence, something quite incapable of giving firm and final direction to the development of a human personality, although they can be indicators of a hardening attitude within us.

Sin We Must Live With

A third and final use of the word "sin" is of great importance to you as parents of a child about to be baptized. This is the expression "original sin." Once again, the ancients saw something in the day-to-day reality of life, the prevalent selfishness in society and whole fabric of human life. They saw masters treating their slaves with contempt, rulers abusing power, peasants cheating their lords, husbands unconcerned about their wives, children who were neglected or who weren't loyal to their parents.

They wondered what to make of this prevalence of sin. The ancient Jewish writers who composed the book of Genesis told a story to express what they had seen. In their story, people from the beginning were selfish, rebellious sinners. From the beginning, sin entered into the fabric of human life. First there was the couple, Adam and Eve, and then their son, Cain, and then all the other selfish, self-willed, self-hating people who created a society of sin, a world ruled by selfishness.

The condition of universal sinfulness described in the book of Genesis and taken for granted by Jesus himself came in time to be called "the original sin"—the sin which has been with us from the beginning, the sin of the whole world.

Jesus promised his followers some freedom from the effects of this sin. This promise is much of what baptism means. It is an incorporation into the mysterious kingdom of God and marks a separation from the powers of sin, the kingdom of darkness, the reign of evil. This is the sense in which we Christians think of the liberation of the baptized child from original sin. It is not some blot upon the child's personality incurred by physical heredity. It is, however, a real thing, an inheritance, not from physical generation, but from being born into a society marred by selfishness, influenced by sin.

Final Word

The whole church, and especially the child's family, makes a pledge at baptism to create in their home a portion of the kingdom of God in which this child may live innocently and happily. Jesus promises his friendship and love. The child, in some way we cannot understand, participates and shares in the death and resurrection of Jesus and emerges from the baptism as one of the brothers or sisters of Jesus destined for and part of the kingdom of God.

Yes, there is sin in this world. There is the reality we call original sin which beckons all people to greed and selfishness and brings violence, war, and oppression. Then, there is the sin we call mortal which we ourselves willingly commit that destroys our lives and those of all who come in contact with us. There are, too, the daily sins, those acts inconsistent with the thrust of our personalities we call venial sin. God will make us one with our brother Jesus and enable us to remain free from the bonds of sin. This new life begins at baptism when the child becomes a member of the community Jesus gave his life to begin.

Ideas for Prayer and Pondering

The short essays that follow are not an essential part of the baptism preparation for parents. You may, however, enjoy reading them to gain a more complete knowledge of topics related to baptism and the Christian life.

Limbo

Some people wonder what happens to the child who dies before being baptized. In the past, some theologians were so impressed by the necessity of baptism that they invented the term "limbo," an idea not found in the Bible. In this "limbo" of theirs, unbaptized infants find only an incomplete happiness, not the happiness of heaven. This idea was never more than an opinion of some theologians. Other theologians have suggested that God, who wants all to be saved, has other ways of saving unbaptized children and these should not concern us. In the end, we simply do not know how God thinks.

Kingdom of God

Jesus told his followers that he had come to inaugurate something different, a time in which the will of God would be done on Earth as it is in heaven. Jesus' life, death, and resurrection began this age in which people, to some degree at least, were unmarked by the selfishness of sin.

Jesus never claimed that his followers were to be the only members of that kingdom, nor that all members of his following would be unmarked by sin. He promised only that his church would somehow be a kind of model of life without sin, a beginning of what Bible writers called "the kingdom of God."

Jesus promised that this kingdom would grow like a mustard seed from tiny beginnings into a great tree. He promised that laced through it would be good and bad, sinner and saint, side by side. But somehow being in this kingdom would be reason enough to be happy and to be ready for the

future where the completion of the kingdom would mean fulfillment in heaven.

The Devil

The baptism ceremony speaks of the devil
when it commands him to depart from the
child. This is difficult to understand. The
child appears to be and is innocent. What
power could the spirit of evil have over
such innocence? Understanding the answer
to this question takes us back to the idea of
original sin, the kingdom of evil, that condition of the whole world brought on by the
sinfulness of our forebears and our con-
temporaries. Because sinfulness is a fact of
life, one easily observed by even the un-
lettered, theology must attempt to explain
it.

The idea that humanity's collective sin
brought about an atmosphere of evil in the
world, a kind of pollution of the human
condition, was the beginning of such an explanation. Then as people began to think of
this condition as a kingdom of evil, of darkness, they wondered if there was not a king
to symbolize and rule over such a reality. In
Jewish thought there evolved such a personality. He was called by many names but
always had two functions.

First, he was the symbol of evil. He
summed up in his personality everything
that is evil, just as a king or president sums
up and symbolizes all that is a nation. But
this person was more than merely a symbolic person. He also gained control over
others by their sinfulness. The more they
became unloving and selfish, the more they
became like him and so the more easily
could he manipulate them. Just as a good
person becomes increasingly sensitive to
God, so the sinner becomes more and more
like the evil one. In this sense the evil one,
the devil, seems to dominate the evil person.

In the baptism ceremony the priest commands the devil to give up all power over
the child and to depart from the child's life.
This is but another way of expressing the
coming into the kingdom of God to the
newly baptized child.

The ceremony of calling upon the devil
to depart from the child is the traditional
exorcism. Often we have heard of the exorcism ceremony only in connection with
bizarre interventions into the life of in-
dividuals, but what is dramatized here is
not so startling. The church asks only that
God protect this child from all that is evil in
the world.

Final Judgment

One writer describes the final judgment
this way. Men and women enter a lovely
room where opposite the door through
which they entered is a smiling, obviously
kind person, happy to see them. The figure
reaches out to embrace them. Those who
have spent a lifetime loving and caring immediately rush into the arms of the friendly
figure. Being children at heart, they embrace this warm and loving parent. But the
sinners, people filled with self-hatred and
self-consciousness, know how deceptive
people can be since they themselves are
filled with deception. Thus, they cannot
spontaneously embrace this smiling figure.
Instead, they turn away. This is their judgment, their hell, their punishment, to be deprived of God forever.

Sin and Sinners

In our courtrooms, we admit that people
who do wrong may not be guilty because
for one reason or other they were unable to
control their actions. The law speaks of insanity, temporary insanity, and mitigating
circumstances. Our courts try to make a
distinction between the wrong done and
the person who did it.

This is also true when we speak of sin. It
is relatively easy to mark certain acts as sinful but impossible for us to state with cer-

tainty that the person who performed them was aware of their evil or free to do otherwise. This is why Jesus warns us not to judge others.

Child abuse, battering women, multiple murders, wartime atrocities, slavery, selling drugs, paying salaries that cannot support a worker's family, and brutal oppression of the poor are clearly sinful acts. We can and must do all in our power to stop them, for they destroy the fabric of society. Yet, even in cases such as these we cannot judge those who commit such sinful actions. God alone knows what led them to behave this way. While society must punish people who do these things, we can never be sure why they acted as they did.

Talking Together

The purpose of this page is to stimulate discussion. A separate, identical sheet is provided for your partner. It is done best after reading all of Part Two. *Read the statements below and check only those you agree with.*

To me, God is:

the Supreme Being who made heaven and Earth	____
the infinitely perfect Spirit	____
someone living and personal	____
the judge of the living and the dead	____
someone I can't understand	____
none of these	____

When I think of God, I think of:

rewards and punishments	____
someone far away	____
a better world	____
a loving friend	____
none of these	____

From the words and phrases listed below, check the three you think best describe sin.

an offense against God	____
breaking a commandment	____
a lack of love	____
a form of selfishness	____
an example of immaturity	____
something we cannot avoid	____
a broken relationship	____
a lack of sensitivity to God or neighbor	____

Now, choose from the list above the three you think are the worst descriptions of sin and place an X next to them.

Spend as much time as you can discussing your answers together. Try to understand not only your partner's thoughts, but his feelings as well. Then take a few moments to pray together about what you discovered in your discussion.

𝔗alking 𝔗ogether

The purpose of this page is to stimulate discussion. A separate identical sheet is provided for each partner. It is done best after reading all of Part Two. *Read the statements below and check only the ones you agree with.*

To me, God is:

the Supreme Being who made heaven and Earth	____
the infinitely perfect Spirit	____
someone living and personal	____
the judge of the living and the dead	____
someone I can't understand	____
none of these	____

When I think of God, I think of:

rewards and punishments	____
someone far away	____
a better world	____
a loving friend	____
none of these	____

From the words and phrases listed below, check the three you think best describe sin.

an offense against God	____
breaking a commandment	____
a lack of love	____
a form of selfishness	____
an example of immaturity	____
something we cannot avoid	____
a broken relationship	____
a lack of sensitivity to God or neighbor	____

Now, choose from the list above the three you think are the worst descriptions of sin and place an X next to them.

Spend as much time as you can discussing your answers together. Try to understand not only your partner's thoughts, but her feelings as well. Then take a few minutes to pray together about what you discovered in your discussion.

PART THREE

Becoming a Christian Parent

From the Ceremony . . .

Celebrant: You have asked to have your children baptized. In doing so you are accepting the responsibility of training them in the practice of the faith. It will be your duty to bring them up to keep God's commandments as Christ taught us, by loving God and our neighbor. Do you clearly understand what you are undertaking?

Parents: We do.

—at the reception of the child for baptism

Celebrant: We anoint you with the oil of salvation
in the name of Christ our Savior;
may he strengthen you with his power,
who lives and reigns for ever and ever.

All: Amen.

—at the anointing before baptism

Celebrant: [child's name], you have become a new creation, and have clothed yourself in Christ.

   See in this white garment the outward sign of your Christian dignity. With your family and friends to help you by word and example, bring that dignity unstained into the everlasting life of heaven.

All: Amen.

—at clothing the child with the white garment

Celebrant: Receive the light of Christ.

Parents and godparents, this light is entrusted to you to be kept burning brightly. These children of yours have been enlightened by Christ. They are to walk always as children of the light. May they keep the flame of faith alive in their hearts. When the Lord comes, may they go out to meet him with all the saints in the heavenly kingdom.

—at the lighting of the baptism candle

Your Child

To focus your thoughts . . .

Please indicate whether you agree or disagree with each statement on this page. Ask your partner to do the same on the page that follows. Both pages are identical. Please do this without discussing the statements. When you have completed your own set of responses, compare your answers with those of your partner and discuss your agreements and disagreements.

1. Parents are responsible for the way their children behave.

      _____Agree   _____Disagree

2. If you raise a child properly, he or she will turn out right.

      _____Agree   _____Disagree

3. In this complicated world of ours, parents have little control over their children.

      _____Agree   _____Disagree

4. I think we will know how to handle our child. We can learn from the mistakes of our parents.

      _____Agree   _____Disagree

5. Good parents make good children.

      _____Agree   _____Disagree

6. It is harder to be a parent today than it was a generation ago.

      _____Agree   _____Disagree

7. The most important gift I can give my child is to continue to grow as a human being and a friend of God.

      _____Agree   _____Disagree

8. Saying no to my child is an important part of parenting.

_____Agree   _____Disagree

9. I am going to need the help of others to be a good parent.

_____Agree   _____Disagree

10. I want the church to play an important part in my parenting.

_____Agree   _____Disagree

After your discussion, read together the essay on the role of parents, pages 47-49.

Your Child

To focus your thoughts . . .

Please indicate whether you agree or disagree with each statement on this page. Ask your partner to do the same on her page. Both pages are identical. Please do this without discussing the statements. When you have completed your own set of responses, compare your answers with those of your partner and discuss your agreements and disagreements.

1. Parents are responsible for the way their children behave.

_____Agree   _____Disagree

2. If you raise a child properly, he or she will turn out right.

_____Agree   _____Disagree

3. In this complicated world of ours, parents have little control over their children.

_____Agree   _____Disagree

4. I think we will know how to handle our child. We can learn from the mistakes of our parents.

_____Agree   _____Disagree

5. Good parents make good children.

_____Agree   _____Disagree

6. It is harder to be a parent today than it was a generation ago.

_____Agree   _____Disagree

7. The most important gift I can give my child is to continue to grow as a human being and a friend of God.

_____Agree   _____Disagree

8. Saying no to my child is an important part of parenting.

_____Agree   _____Disagree

9. I am going to need the help of others to be a good parent.

_____Agree   _____Disagree

10. I want the church to play an important part in my parenting.

_____Agree   _____Disagree

After your discussion, read together the essay on the role of parents, pages 47-49.

Parents' Role

 Being a parent is an awesome responsibility, because parents share in God's most important work, a task that will last a lifetime and reach into heaven itself. Your child will need your help for years to come, as you yourself perhaps still depend on your own parents in many different ways.

Our Culture's Myth

There is a myth about parents, one that is everywhere in our culture. This myth lays all responsibility for children's development on the shoulders of their parents. It pictures children as totally passive persons who absorb all their values and attitudes from their parents and make little or no contribution to the development of their own personalities. Parents are blamed for all that goes wrong in their children's lives.

There is, of course, some truth in this. If, however, you are the parents of more than one child or if you have brothers or sisters of your own, you know that life is not that simple. From birth, each person has a distinctive personality, a personality that can never be completely mastered by anyone.

Parents have a responsibility to provide a healthy environment for their children, which will make it easier for them to make good decisions. A loving, thoughtful, and religious home is important for a child's personal growth. Yet the time will come when you as parents must stand aside and allow your children to decide for themselves. Even the best of environments and the most loving parents can never be fully responsible for the outcome of their children's lives.

Giving Your Child the Best

As parents, you want to give your child the very best. Let's look at some of the attitudes and things you can and should provide.

Of course, there are the basics: food, shelter, physical care, education, and good companions. Even in these most fundamental human needs, balance is required. To give your children too much food or food that is too rich can create health problems or leave them with a lifelong addiction to overeating. To live in a neighborhood that has no poor people and no one who is elderly can teach a child that everyone in the world should be youthful and rich. An education that produces fine academic standards may miss the more subtle needs for companionship and association with different kinds of people. Good companions are important, but to be deprived of all contact with anything unpleasant can leave a child unprepared for many of life's problems.

From the beginning, parents are called upon to search for a balanced life for themselves and their children. The more deeply they care about Jesus and the community of the church, the more likely it is that they will discover practical, concrete answers to questions about everyday problems.

Happy Home

A more subtle gift parents can give their child is their own loving relationship. Nothing breeds growth and self-confidence in a child like living with parents deeply in love with each other. This is not always possible, of course, since both father and mother must want such a relationship and be capable of it. Even when parents cannot live happily together, they must put aside their differences as best they can when dealing with their children. A loving and consistent relationship is usually possible in the most difficult circumstances.

Transmitting Faith

All Christians know that parents cannot impose their own faith upon their children. Faith is a free gift from God. Both the Bible and the experience of generations of Christian people make this point clear. Yet parents do have a role in preparing children to believe in Jesus. They help their children feel at home in the community of faith. As parents pray with the community and at home, children sense that prayer is a normal and natural part of life. They imitate their parents' prayer even when they do not yet understand it.

Parents also explain to children the words and symbols used by the community. They see to it that their children grow in a knowledge of these words and customs as they mature. A Catholic school or a religion class in a parish helps them with this work. As children grow older, they begin to feel comfortable with the community because they use the same language and the same symbols as it does.

A knowledge of the community demands some understanding of its past, where it came from, and who its heroes are. Parents tell children stories of our Christian past: stories from Scripture, stories of the saints, and personal stories, too. This accumulation of stories profoundly influences growing children. They become proud to be a part of a community with roots stretching back through the centuries. Being proud of the church is an important step toward wanting to be a member of it in adult life.

Finally, parents patiently explain the expectations of the community, which are spelled out in rules and customs. At times they may seem unreasonable to the youngster, but parents tell their children how these rules helped them and how they enhanced their own growth and happiness.

Much of what parents do is done unselfconsciously. As parents live their faith and create an authentically Christian lifestyle, they prepare the ground for the seed of faith to grow. While God gives the free gift of faith, parents help nurture and strengthen that gift. Children remain free to accept or reject it.

Your Personality

You cannot be a good parent without being a good person. As you grow into deeper relationships with others, with your family, and with the community of faith, you become a more mature and stronger human person. This growth is reflected in your role as a parent. The more mature you become, the easier your parenting task becomes.

Parenting itself will call upon you to grow. Rising to feed an infant in the middle of the night, anxiously nursing a sick child, attempting to cope with a child's stubborn personality, and accepting the limits of your child's gifts—all will push you toward a more selfless lifestyle. This can make you a more mature and more religious person.

Here, as in all aspects of human life, there are two extremes to be avoided. Some parents deny all aspects of their life except parenting. They become so completely taken up with their children that they neglect the rest of life. They attempt to form their own identity through their child. Such a way of life becomes neurotic and damages both child and parent. There is more to adult life than parenting.

On the other hand, some parents grow to resent the restrictions children place on them. They avoid their role as parents as much as they can. Babysitters replace parents. Gifts replace time spent lovingly with a child. A job often becomes more important than the key role of helping a child grow. Children understand this, even when they cannot find words to express it, and harbor a deep resentment at being extra baggage in a family. Both the child and the parents suffer when a child is neglected.

Neglected children often punish their parents by behaving badly and ultimately by rejecting their parents as their parents once rejected them.

Final Word

No one can draw a map for the new parent. Life has too many unexpected and surprising turns. No two children are alike; no two mothers or fathers are alike either. The growth that parents and children experience together is always unique.

In setting out on this road, you bring with you all of your past experiences and the inner depths of the person you have already become. God promises to be with you day in and day out, helping you grow and become a more effective parent. The community of faith, too, wants to be a part of your parenting. It will reach out to you at each stage of your child's life and at each stage of your own.

Symbols in the Baptism Rite

Much of the beauty of the baptism ceremony is found in the rich symbols used to express the community's concern for your child. These symbols often speak more profoundly than words can. They have roots in our distant past and yet speak softly to the most modern person at the ceremony.

Water

The first symbol is, of course, water, and the most important thing about water is that it supports all life. Anyone touched by the ecological movement knows how important water is to human life. In the baptism ceremony water is important, too, because it reminds you that your child will be sustained in a new and different kind of life, the life Jesus promised, as God's own child.

There is another meaning to this symbol, one lost on many of us today unless we have lived though a serious flood. Ancient people always feared water even as they depended on it. When water came rushing over the river banks to destroy their fragile civilizations, it was a sign of chaos, destruction, and death.

When early Christians saw a child plunged into the water, they held their breath and remembered that this young person was dying with Christ to the old world order, the age of sin and selfishness, which they called the kingdom of darkness. When the child emerged from the water unharmed, they remembered that the child was being raised up with Christ, unharmed, to a new kind of life, an age of love and kindness, which they called the kingdom of light or the reign of God.

Today some of this symbolism is lost because we rarely plunge the children into a pool of water but instead pour a little water on their foreheads. Yet the meaning is the same. We are asked to remember that this child, your child, is passing from an ordinary human life into the beginning of something new, a life as God's own child.

The Cross

One of the most touching ceremonies in the baptism liturgy occurs when the priest makes a small sign of the cross on the child's forehead and asks parents and godparents to do the same. The whole Christian community reaches into its past for a symbol to portray its deepest belief about life. That symbol is the cross of Jesus.

As the cross is traced upon the child's forehead, Christians remember that Jesus tasted the fullness of human life and will be with this child forever. Together with Jesus, this child will touch and taste all of life's beauties and sorrows. Because Jesus is present, the child will never be alone.

Lighted Candle

A candle was once people's most common source of light during the dark night hours. For Christians it became a symbol of Jesus who brought us out of the kingdom of darkness into the kingdom of light. The drama of Jesus, the bringer of light, is played out magnificently during the Easter Vigil Mass when a large candle, a symbol of Jesus, is lit and its flame then used to kindle the candles of all present.

In the baptism ceremony this dramatic moment is recalled as you the parents are given a lighted candle, another reminder that through baptism your child passes from the kingdom of darkness into the kingdom of light.

Oil

Twice during the baptism ceremony your child will be anointed with oil. This anointing is a very ancient ceremony. In ages gone by, oil was a healing remedy and a sign of power. Kings, priests, and prophets were anointed, as were the sick, so that they might be strengthened and healed.

Entering the community of faith is an important moment in the life of your child, one that calls for future strength and dedication. By using oil, the church dramatizes its prayer that this child will be strengthened by God and by the prayer of the whole community. Oil also recalls to us that one day in the future the Christian community will once again anoint this young person, on confirmation day. Again, that anointing, like this one, will be a prayer for greater strength to live out the demands of the gospel of Jesus in everyday life.

White Garment

In earlier days all who were baptized, young and old, were clothed in a long white garment, which they wore the week after their baptism. The white garment reminded all in the community that these new Christians were clothed in Christ, that in a very real sense he shared their lives, and they his. They were urged to carry that new life with them and to keep it unstained until the day they met the Lord in heaven.

Today we remember that custom by dressing infants in a baptism dress and small children in white clothes. Toward the end of the ceremony, a small symbolic robe is placed over the dress, a reminder to all who witness the ceremony that we are called to live simply and sinlessly, even in the midst of a cruel and chaotic world.

Godparents

Godparents, too, are a symbol, a sign of the whole church's concern for this new child. In days when parents often died before a child reached maturity, godparents promised to take on the responsibility of rearing the child in the faith if anything happened to the parents. Today they promise to help parents in their task as Christian mothers and fathers.

Godparents are to be role models for the child. Therefore you must choose godparents with care. What is important is not so much how closely they are related to the child as how closely they seem related to the Lord. Since godparents represent the best of the Christian family, they should live out its ideals in their daily lives.

Symbols

Through symbols such as water, cross, oil, candle, white garments, and the godparents themselves, the church speaks to you about the life your child will live in the Christian community. What better way to begin your role as Christian parents than to ponder the ageless symbols of the church and to understand both the burden and the promise of being parents to your newly baptized child!

Ideas for Prayer and Pondering

The short essays that follow are not an essential part of the baptism preparation for parents. You may, however, enjoy reading them to gain a more complete knowledge of topics related to baptism and the Christian life.

Selecting a Name

Nothing is more personal to us than our names. The name of a person is the symbol of all that is unique and incommunicable about an individual. One's name sums up who and what he or she is.

An old Catholic custom is to name the newborn after a saint. The purpose is to invoke one of the holy men or women from the past as a special patron or protector of the new life at its beginning. Yet it is more. Naming a child after a saint also gives him or her a sense of history, a sense of tradition. By giving children the names of the great people of the past, we hope to awaken in them a realization that they walk with Jesus as did so many who went before them.

Children become curious about their names. They desire to know why they are named as they are. They want to understand who bore the name before they did, who gave it glory. Their name is something special, even sacred, to them. They are not certain why, but their names have a profound impact on them.

Catholic parents approach the idea of naming a child, then, with great interest. For many, the name is a link with the family's past, a father's name, a mother's, or uncle's. For others, it is a sign of what they hope the child will become: another Francis, a new Saint Angela. For still others, the name is a sign of what they have left behind: their old ways and their old family traditions. Thus the many different names chosen.

While there is nothing in baptism itself that demands the choice of a saint's name or a Christian name, there is a tradition which beckons one to follow it. There is nothing magic about the choice of a name, yet the impact of that name on the formation of the child's future should give parents a reason to consider it seriously.

Names of the saints exist by the hundreds. Careful parents will think about the many good people who have gone before, both in the church's tradition and in the family heritage, and find one name that seems to fit the present reality of life and give that as a gift from the past to their new son or daughter.

Baptism During Mass

To sense and feel the full impact and beauty of your child's baptism, you should try to have the sacrament celebrated during one of the Sunday liturgies. Many parishes offer this opportunity if their Sunday Mass schedule is not too crowded. There you will be surrounded by the community of believers where everyone will witness the ceremony of dedicating your child to God and renewing your own baptism promises. The whole family of faith will pray on your behalf. You will be swept up in the warmth and concern of all God's people as they welcome the newest member into the community.

Talking Together

The purpose of this page is to stimulate discussion. A separate, identical sheet is provided for your partner. It is done best after reading all of Part Three.

When you think about your role as parent, what do you look forward to most?

_____

_____

_____

_____

_____

When you think about your role as parent, what makes you uneasy?

_____

_____

_____

_____

_____

Spend as much time as you can discussing your answers together. Try to understand not only your partner's thoughts, but his feelings as well. Then take a few moments to pray together about what you discovered in your discussion.

Talking Together

The purpose of this page is to stimulate discussion. A separate, identical sheet is provided for each parent. It is done best after reading all of Part Three.

When you think about your role as parent, what do you look forward to most?

_____

_____

_____

_____

_____

_____

When you think about your role as parent, what makes you uneasy?

_____

_____

_____

_____

_____

Spend as much time as you can discussing your answers together. Try to understand not only your partner's thoughts, but her feelings as well. Then take a few moments to pray together about what you discovered in your discussion.

PART FOUR

Preparing for the Ceremony

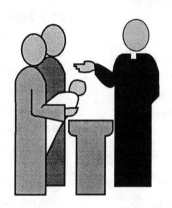

Family Preparations

Life is one small episode after another. If we wish to make one stand out from all the others, we have to invest it with solemnity and importance. Thus, parents have to avoid making baptism a "rush job," which takes little more time and attention than the ceremony itself. With some attention to preparation, though, the child's baptism can loom large as one of the central moments of married life.

Here are some suggestions for adding importance to the baptism of your child.

1. Take the time to select the readings for the ceremony, if it will take place outside of Mass. (See the description of the baptism rite on pages 60-62.) Then, arrange to have members of the family act as the readers.

2. If you have children old enough to be more than spectators, let them be part of the ceremony. One might hold the little baptism garment, another carry the oils for the priest, etc. An older child might well be one of the readers.

3. Make a baptism banner with the other children or by yourselves. This can be made easily by cutting out baptism symbols and the child's name from colored felt and gluing them on a large piece of felt of contrasting color. The banner may be displayed during the ceremony and then put up in the child's room.

4. You might ask a grandparent or other relative to embroider a wall hanging with the date of baptism and the child's name. This could be permanently mounted in a prominent place in your home. (A good source of graphic ideas are baptism greeting cards.)

5. Arrange for a few snapshots or a video of the child, yourselves, the godparents, the priest or deacon, and the entire group. Carefully label the pictures in a sacramental book in which you will later add pictures of your child's first communion, confirmation, marriage, and other sacramental moments.

6. Make the baptism garment for the ceremony. The garment should be white and can be decorated with baptism symbols. A simple way to make an infant's garment is to cut a 20-inch diameter circle of material with a 6-inch circle cut out of the center. (See illustration below.) Bind the raw edges with bias tape and embroider; iron on or glue on baptism symbols. The garment easily slips over the child's head at the proper time during the ceremony, symbolizing the new life received in baptism. For older children you may make a simple cape.

7. Decorate the candle to be lighted during the baptism ceremony. This can easily be prepared and kept for other special occasions in the child's life, even a yearly celebration of his or her baptism day or birthday. Start with a white candle large enough to decorate with the child's name, the date, and symbols.

First, cover the candle with a coat of clear acrylic and allow to dry. Next apply decorations with acrylic paints available in small tubes and jars. When the paint is dry, cover with another coat of clear acrylic. (See illustration on page 50.)

8. Write a letter to your child and put it in a safe place to be read at confirmation time or just before marriage. In the letter describe your feelings at this moment of your child's baptism.

9. Make a donation of money, or better, time and effort to some worthy cause in the child's name. Some parishes preserve the custom of making an offering to the priest or deacon who performs the ceremony.

10. If you have other children, take the time to explain just what will happen at the ceremony. Tell them about the candle, the water, the oil, and the other symbols. If possible, arrange for a family member to be with the children during the ceremony so that you will be free to enjoy it.

11. Plan a celebration for all who will attend the baptism. With the help of the other children, decorate the house.

12. Write a family prayer to be said just before or after the ceremony. Let the officiating priest or deacon know of your plans to read this prayer together.

In these and other simple ways, the church ceremony of baptism can take on greater meaning and importance in the life of your family.

The Rite of Baptism

AN OUTLINE

The ceremony of the baptism of a child is described on these pages, 60-62; it is not the rite itself. If you wish to read the full text of the church's rite before your child's ceremony, ask a member of the parish staff for a copy.

 The rite used to baptize children today has its roots in symbols that date from the time before Jesus and in prayers that have been said since the dawn of Christianity. Each of the eight parts of the ceremony says something special about human life and God's desire to uplift and make it holy.

1. A Word of Welcome

Jesus once said, "Where two or three are gathered in my name, I am there among them." Parents, godparents, the child (or children) to be baptized, the priest or deacon who represents the worldwide church, and both family and friends—all gather in Jesus' name and so he, too, is present for this special day.

Speaking for the whole church, the priest welcomes each person present and asks the parents two simple questions:

• what name they wish to give their child and
• why they have come to the church today.

When they answer that their reason for coming to the church is to baptize their child, the priest reminds them of the great task that lies before them, sharing their faith with their child (or children). He asks them if they understand what it means when they respond that they do; he asks the godparents if they understand their role as the parents' helpers.

The priest then turns to the child and in one of the most touching of all the church's ceremonies, makes a tiny cross on each child's forehead as a sign that they now belong to Jesus. Parents and godparents imitate what the priest has done, for Jesus is present in everyone. With these simple ceremonies the welcome is complete.

2. Listening to God's Word

We believe that Jesus, his Father, and the Spirit are present with us, as are the valiant men and women who went before us in faith. We listen to God's word found in the Bible and then turn to God and the saints in prayer.

The family and the priest may select one Bible reading to be read at the ceremony. Or they may follow the Lectionary readings for that Sunday's Mass and include the three readings, a responsorial psalm, and an Alleluia verse. Some of the Bible readings often used at baptism are:

Old Testament

Exodus 17:3–7	Ezekiel 36:24–28
Ezekiel 47:1–9,12	

New Testament

Matthew 22:35–40	John 4:5–4
Matthew 28:18–20	John 7:37b–39a
Mark 1:9–11	John 15:1–11
Mark 10:13–16	Romans 6:3–5
Mark 12:29b–34	Romans 8:28–32

John 3:1–6   1 Corinthians 12:12–13
John 6:44–47   Galatians 3:26–28
John 9:1–7   Ephesians 4:1–6
John 19:31–35   1 Peter 2:4–5,9–10

Suggested Responsorial Psalms:
Psalm 23:1–3a, 3b–4, 5, 6
Response: The Lord is my shepherd:
                 I shall not want. (Psalm 23:1)

Psalm 27:1, 4, 8b–9c, 13–14
Response: The Lord is my light and my
                 salvation. (Psalm 27:1)

Readings Often Used as an Alleluia Verse:
    John 3:16   Ephesians 4:5–6
    John 8:12   2 Timothy 1:10
    John 14:6   1 Peter 2–9

After listening to God's word and at times to a short homily, we turn to prayer. The form of the prayer is that used at Sunday Mass at the Prayer of the Faithful. The prayer itself is a series of petitions begging God to be with the child (or children) about to be baptized, with their parents and godparents, and with all who are struggling to live out their baptism commitment.

In baptism the child (or children) will be initiated into the great family we know as the communion of saints. Our family stretches to the farthest ends of creation and includes those alive today and those faithful men, women, and children who have already died. Aware of this, the priest intones the names of a few of the heroic men and women who have gone before us, people like Mary, John the Baptist, Joseph, and perhaps the patron saints of the child (children) about to be baptized. Everyone responds "Pray for us" as the priest calls on each saint by name.

3. Prayer of Exorcism
On page 34 is an explanation of why this ancient prayer is present in the ritual. The priest asks God in our name to protect the child (or children) from all evil just as we pray in the Lord's Prayer, "Lead us not into temptation, but deliver us from evil."

4. Anointing
Anointing with oil is a sacred act of prayer. Long ago, priests, prophets, and kings were anointed, and now the child (or children) soon to be united with Jesus through baptism is anointed and thus shares in these three roles with him. The priest prays that God will strengthen the child (or children) in life's struggle that lies ahead.

5. Blessing the Baptism Water
The priest then blesses the baptism water, recalling from the Easter Vigil ceremony that the water symbolizes the womb of the church from which new Christian life will spring. Of course, when the water has already been blessed, this prayer is not said.

6. Profession of Faith
The priest now asks the parents and godparents whether they themselves profess the belief of the church. He may ask this in many different ways; the most ancient and perhaps most beautiful way is based on the Apostles Creed and put in the form of questions to which all may respond, "I do believe."

Do you believe in God, the Father almighty,
    creator of heaven and earth?

Do you believe in Jesus Christ,
    his only son, our Lord,
who was born of the Virgin Mary,

was crucified, died and was buried,
rose from the dead,
and is now seated at the right hand of
the Father?

Do you believe in the Holy Spirit,
the holy Catholic Church,
the communion of saints,
the forgiveness of sins,
the resurrection of the body,
and the life everlasting?

Conclusion:
This is our faith. This is the faith of the
Church. We are proud to profess it, in
Christ Jesus our Lord.

7. The Baptism

The priest now asks the parents and
godparents if they want the child (or
children) to be baptized. When they
answer yes, he pours water over the
child's forehead and says, "I baptize
you in the name of the Father, and of
the Son, and of the Holy Spirit."

8. Concluding Ceremonies

Anointing with Chrism:
Centuries ago and in some countries
today, children were confirmed at this
moment. In most parts of the world today, this sacrament, part of the initiation rite, is held at a later time in
the children's life but the anointing
with chrism remains in the ceremony.

The Baptism Garment:
In the third century when adults were
received into the church, they donned
long white robes and wore them for a
week as a public sign that they were
entering a new kind of life. We main-
tain that symbolism in the white garment baptized children wear.

The Lighted Candle:
When people were baptized at the
Easter Vigil Mass they received a candle lit from the great Easter candle in a
darkened church, a symbol that their
faith was a share in the faith of Jesus,
the Light of the World, and his
church. This ancient symbol remains
in our ceremony.

The Lord's Prayer:
Together, all join as God's family in
saying the prayer Jesus taught us.

The Final Blessing:
The priest asks God to bless the mother, the father, and the child (or children). To each of his prayers we
answer, "Amen."

Parents' Prayer

Lord, help us with our task of parenting.

Help us be full of case-hardened strength
And yet, never far from feeling.

Help us be free and full of heady joy
And yet, not unaware of real life.

And most of all, Lord, let us be together—
Together strong,
Together wise,
Together free and full of joy.

Let this love we feel for each other
be the love we share as parents. Amen.

Of Related Interest...

Celebrating Sacraments
Baptism: Welcome to the Christian Community
Charles Keating
This video for parents and sponsors helps viewers appreciate the depth of the sacrament as it stimulates confidence in their ability to impart Christian values to the newly baptized. Also available in Spanish.
15 minutes, $39.95

At Home with the Sacraments
Baptism
Peg Bowman
This book is for parents preparing to have their child baptized in the Catholic Church. It explores the tradition, ritual and symbols of the sacrament, informing parents and supporting them in their roles as spiritual models for their child.
ISBN: 0-89622-478-3, 48 pp, $3.95

Sacraments Alive
Their History, Significance, and Celebration
Sandra DeGidio
This book updates readers' understanding of the sacraments as they are celebrated today.
ISBN: 0-89622-489-9, 160 pp, $9.95

Catholic Customs and Traditions
A Popular Guide
Greg Dues
How did the rosary originate? What meaning do certain colors have in Catholic worship? Why are oils important? These and other practices are explained in this revised and expanded edition.
ISBN: 0-89622-515-1, 224 pp, $9.95

Available at religious bookstores or from:

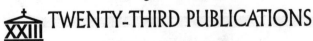

XXIII TWENTY-THIRD PUBLICATIONS

1-800-321-0411

E-Mail:ttpubs@aol.com